Gertie's Worry Cloud

by

Izzy Unger-Finn

RGP

Really Good Press

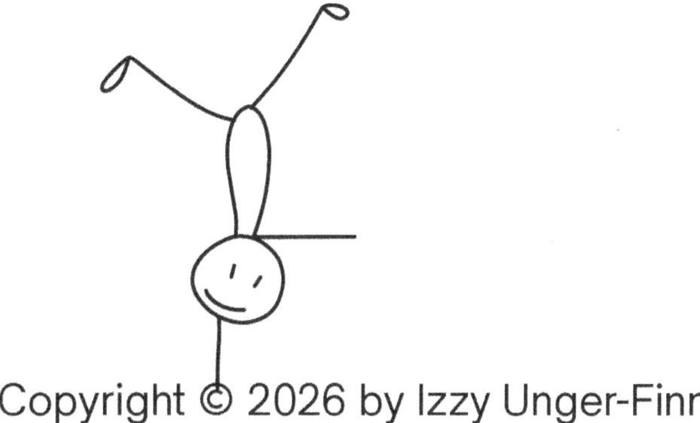

To Mark: my husband, my soulmate, and...my ever-vigilant editor.

Characters

Gertie
Anna, Gertie's Foster Mom
Beeba Lou
And...
The Worry Cloud

Early Monday morning,
Gertie woke up,
but something felt very, very
strange...

Right above her head floated a small gray cloud.

Gertie stared at it...

And stared at it...

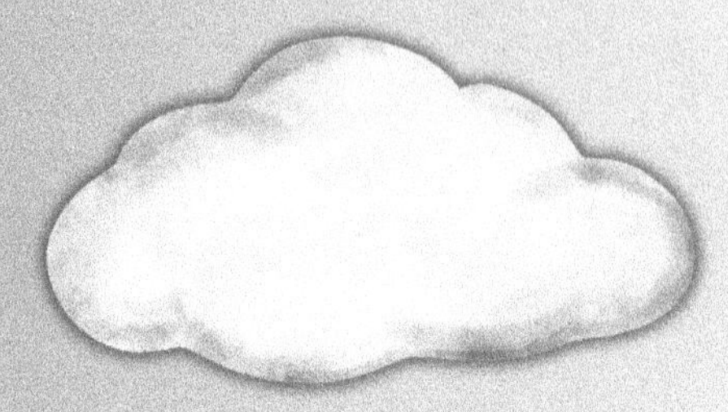

Gertie hadn't seen it before, but somehow she knew what it was.

It was a worry.

And it had formed a cloud over her head.

The cloud was there because today was her first day at her new school.

And Gertie had lots of worries in her mind!

What if no one wants to sit with her at lunch?
MILK

what if nobody likes her??

What if everything feels all WRONG
all the time and doesn't stop??

The more Gertie thought about
these things, the bigger the worry
cloud grew!

And grew....

Worry clouds are like that.
They don't give up easily.

At breakfast, Gertie wasn't hungry.

"Is that a worry cloud I see?" Gertie's foster-mother, whose name is Anna, gently asked.

"You can see it??" Gertie asked
surprised.

"I get worry clouds too," Anna said. "Everyone gets them sometimes. See mine? Now, I am worried about YOUR worries!"

"What do you do with your worry clouds?"
Gertie wanted to know.

"Well," Anna said, "First I give my worry a name."

Gertie thought hard. "Hmmm...my worry's name is...New School!" she said.

"That's a big worry. And it makes a
lot of sense," Anna said.

"Let's try this!" Anna said.
"We'll take three big breaths together.
In through your nose...
then out through your mouth.
Ready?"
New School

one...

Two...

Three!

"I still feel it, but not as much," said
Gertie.

"That's okay," said Anna. "Worries don't
disappear all at once. But breathing tells
your body — you are safe."

Then, Anna handed Gertie a piece of paper and some crayons. "Sometimes," she said, "drawing your worry makes it feel smaller."

Gertie picked up the gray crayon and began to draw.

She drew the cloud. She drew herself underneath it. And then... she drew herself smiling." I made it smaller," Gertie whispered, "on the paper."

When it was time to leave, Gertie put on her backpack. The worry cloud came along too. But it was just a little bit smaller than before.

The school was big. The hallways were loud. The worry cloud puffed up again.

Gertie took a deep breath. In through her
nose. Out through her mouth.
"I am safe," she whispered to herself.

Then a girl with a bright yellow backpack stopped beside her. "Are you new?" she asked, with a smile. "I'm Beeba Lou. I'll show you where our classroom is."

Gertie felt something warm flutter in her chest. She took Beeba Lou's hand. And for just a moment... she forgot about the cloud.

At lunch, Gertie and Beeba Lou sat together.
They both liked dogs. They both hated
mushrooms on pizza.
Gertie giggled for the first time all day. And
the worry cloud got very small.

When the bell rang at the end of the day,
Gertie walked outside. Anna was waiting
with a warm smile. "How was it?"
she asked.

Gertie thought for a moment. "It was hard at first," she said honestly. "But then... it got better."

Anna looked above Gertie's head. "What happened to your worry cloud?" she asked. Gertie looked up. They both gasped.

The worry cloud was almost gone. Just
the tiniest wisp remained — like the last
bit of smoke from a blown-out birthday
candle.

"Will it come back?" Gertie asked.
"Maybe sometimes," said Anna gently.
"But now you know — worry clouds don't
last forever. And you are never too
small to make them shrink."

That night, Gertie drew one more
picture. A little girl. A tiny cloud. And a
great big smile. She wrote at the
bottom in her very best letters:
I can do hard things!

A Note for Parents, Caregivers & Educators

Worry and the anxiety it provokes, is a normal and healthy part of childhood — but for some children, anxiety can *feel overwhelming* and hard to manage alone. Gertie's Worry Cloud is designed to open conversations about *feelings* in a safe, gentle way.

Here are a *few* ways to use this book:

- After reading, ask your child: "Have you ever had a worry cloud? What did it look like and *feel* like?"
- Practice the breathing exercise together — in through the nose, out through the mouth and see how the body responds.
- Encourage your child to draw or name their worries, just like Gertie.
- Remind them that ALL *feelings* are okay — it's what we do with them that matters

If your child's worries *feel* persistent or are interfering with daily life, consider speaking with your pediatrician or a *licensed* child therapist.

You are never too small, or too big, to ask for help.

WEBSITES

The Kids Mental Health Foundation
Mental health is as important as physical health and this organization has more reserouces than you'll probably ever need,
https://www.kidsmentalhealthfoundation.org/

The American Academy of Child & Adolescent Psychiatry
https://www.aacap.org/

American Academy of Pediatrics
https://www.healthychildren.org/English/family-life/family-dynamics/Pages/help-your-child-manage-fears-and-anxieties.aspx

---

Coping Cat Parents

Don't let the name fool you. This website has nothing to do with cats and everything to do with kids struggling with anxiety. With everything from Camp Cope-a-Lot to Child Anxiety Tales, it's truly a gem amidst the growing body of material supporting kid's mental health.

Coping Skills for Kids

Print a Coping Skills checklist & deep breathing exercises, watch a podcast, explore books and resources. There are just a few

If you enjoyed reading
Gertie's Worry Cloud,
please consider leaving a review on Amazon or
Goodreads. Good reviews tell the Great Algorithm that
you *like* us, prompting it to send more readers our way
so they can also discover Gertie.

Your support is everything!

Gertie & I Thank You!

www.IzzyUngerFinn.com